"Chicago-based poet and educator Kevin Coval has one of the strongest and most long-standing literary visions in the city."

—*Chicago Tribune*

"[Coval is] Chicago's unofficial poet laureate."

—**NPR**

"In *Everything Must Go*, Kevin Coval taps into nostalgia familiar as a former lover's cologne. Colorful characters come alive in his prose. They make you laugh and the documentation of a neighborhood undergoing gentrification makes you wince. This book is dope."

—**Natalie Moore**, author of *The South Side: A Portrait of Chicago and American Segregation*

"*Everything Must Go* is a requiem, a novel in verse, a history of a neighborhood, and a city that time has put through a fun-house mirror. It is powered by the love and friction of people building lives that fill out the shape of a neighborhood—and the loss they feel when the neighborhood's new shape no longer fits them. Whether or not you lived through the Wicker Park of the 1990s, *Everything Must Go* will have something to say to you, something to teach you, and something to make you remember."

—**Daniel Kay Hertz**, author of *The Battle of Lincoln Park: Urban Renewal and Gentrification in Chicago*

"Kevin Coval is an architect of ghosts. His poems salvage, memorialize, and rectify the body of a city. Positioned beside illustrations from Langston Allston, these poems leave no ghost untold, and no building untouched. It's a book that brings attention to the smoldering of gentrification, and thoughtfully mourns its feasting. A must read for anyone sitting in the present, having recently escaped the mouth of the past."

—**Kara Jackson**, National Youth Poet Laureate

"A vibrant yet solemn portrait of Chicago's Wicker Park in the 90s, this collection examines gentrification and commemorates what gets lost in the process."

—*Lit Hub*'s Most Anticipated Books of 2019

"[Coval writes] fascinating, beautiful poems."

—**Trevor Noah**, *The Daily Show*

"Kevin Coval made me understand what it is to be a poet, what it is to be an artist, and what it is to serve the people."

—**Chance the Rapper**

"I'm reading these great poems right now. I make sure I find time to support artists that help other artists. Turmeric is good for your inflamation for your information. This book is great in detail about human life. It's very interesting to a human being with unlimited emotions. I recommend this book with black seed oil!"

—**Sharkula**

EVERYTHING MUST GO

The BreakBeat Poets Series

ABOUT THE BREAKBEAT POETS SERIES

The BreakBeat Poets series, curated by Kevin Coval and Nate Marshall, is committed to work that brings the aesthetic of hip-hop practice to the page. These books are a cipher for the fresh, with an eye always to the next. We strive to center and showcase some of the most exciting voices in literature, art, and culture.

BREAKBEAT POETS SERIES TITLES INCLUDE:

The BreakBeat Poets: New American Poetry in the Age of Hip-Hop, edited by Kevin Coval, Quraysh Ali Lansana, and Nate Marshall

This is Modern Art: A Play, Idris Goodwin and Kevin Coval

The BreakBeat Poets Vol 2: Black Girl Magic, edited by Mahogany L. Browne, Jamila Woods, and Idrissa Simmonds

Human Highlight, Idris Goodwin and Kevin Coval

On My Way to Liberation, H. Melt

Black Queer Hoe, Britteney Black Rose Kapri

Citizen Illegal, José Olivarez

Graphite, Patricia Frazier

The BreakBeat Poets Vol 3: Halal If You Hear Me, edited by Fatimah Asghar and Safia Elhillo

Commando, E'mon Lauren

Build Yourself a Boat, Camonghne Felix

Milwaukee Avenue, Kevin Coval, illustrated by Langston Allston

Bloodstone Cowboy, Kara Jackson

Can I Kick It?, Idris Goodwin

EVERYTHING MUST GO

The Life and Death of an American Neighborhood

kevin coval

illustrated by langston allston

Haymarket Books
Chicago, Illinois

Published in 2019 by
Haymarket Books
P.O. Box 180165
Chicago, IL 60618
www.haymarketbooks.org

ISBN: 978-1-64259-175-0

Distributed to the trade in the US through Consortium Book Sales and
Distribution (www.cbsd.com) and internationally through Ingram Publisher
Services International (www.ingramcontent.com).

This book was published with the generous support of Lannan Foundation and
Wallace Action Fund.

Cover design by Langston Allston and Bryanna McNeal.
Interior design by Langston Allston and Jamie Kerry.

Printed in the United States.

This is not the rebuilding of cities. This is the sacking of cities.
—Jane Jacobs

Contents

A Brief History

they came
made a village
an alley to play in
a street to wander
a growing mass
new corners / comers
just off the boat / train
on the Ave. just out
the loop, off the bus
stop. fight for a job
for pay, for food, a spot
to stay in the country
when the country
was a saloon. a sanctuary
for George Marcus Coval
fleeing Ukrainians
trying to kill his family.

the streets Algren slunk drunk on.
when men were scattered & scared.
women too. golden-armed dropouts;
fathers, barmaids, prostitutes.
Native then Irish, Russian, Polish
Puerto Rican, Mexican, Black.
then everything shut down.
bungalow ambitions shipped
elsewheres.

the kennedy sliced the belly
in two. just like that
cut from the loop. the gold
coast, jobs just east, the block
its own prison staring Cabrini
in its eye.

                    no white person
with money wanted
anything downtown
anything other.
didn't want someone
to step over on the way
to the suburbs, the grocery
fast food mcmansions
then stop.
          hammer time.

          the tasteless taste shift
raiders of the last art
mobbed the block, returned to the city
in hordes. redline ward wand-wavers
waivers, TIFs, democratic party tiffs
tips, investments. invest-
ors, a bare-brick cafe.
outposts, pastlines
gerrymandered galleries, records
erased, reckless
corner stores closed.

          the sons & daughters
of farmers went to art school.
blue collars turned plaid. sub
-urbanites with failed dreams
want what america promised:
heroin & cheap rent & space to think
& nod off in a basement. shifts to make
shit. squatters excavate spaces. the place is
a house party, turned rave, turned electro
turned Red Dog, with white noses
white powder to white powers.
a whole country waging
                    a war
on drugs, a commercial
boom industry for private prisons

                    a war
america is
destined to win
                    a war
waged in these
Division Streets
                    a war
in this village
this wicked park
                    a war
to stop the mix
to stop workers from mixing
so intimate they can smell
each other's cooking.

1750 w. Haddon

1

the doorframe's round like a half moon.
round like doors in the ghetto in venice
an architectural wink to let jews know
what home was safe to enter.

it musta looked this way in 1906
when George, who died of a heart attack
before we met, walked in & out as a boy
making his way in this new city / country / century.

how many times, i've walk this block
unknowingly. i moved to Wicker
at the beginning of its end. rotated around
this street & doorframe my whole life
a magnet, an axis, a grand sun drawn
without explanation or nation.

2

Aunt Joyce raised me.
den mother to the Second City.
we're having blueberry pancakes
at a cafe on Division that's come & gone
so often the street's a revolving door.

as if she told me for the thousandth time:
you know your grandfather lived a few blocks from here.

we went, the two of us, in the end of summer
as fall wraps a light coat around your shoulders.
after the waitress cleared plates, syrup still stuck
on my hand. my aunt, the best comedian in the house
of Belushi, as i'm all sentimental, tears ready to fly, says

yeah, not so much to look at.

3

if i love you   i'll bring you here

4

George met bubbe Pearl at a dance in the community center.
he'd have to take a streetcar to see her again. she was from out west
a thousand cousins stuffed onto a block in North Lawndale. he'd sink
in his seat when crossing the neighborhood cuz he was solo in a ward
of gangs & didn't want anyone to know he fell in love with a Polack.

5

of course, i don't remember
why we were fighting, but we were
& it was before you left what i wasn't sure you would
& there you were just sitting on the stoop
where George came to live. this safe zone, you said
you came here to be close to me. you went to the spot
i go to tether me to earth again, a line to my body
its history, where i revolve on axis. you have access
have broken in & sat & laughed with me on the landing
in the light where my life landed, you went right to the spot
i go, a spot that's not my home, but is my ancestral land.

no one here has ever
been to the lake.
a giant poster of Travis Bickle
waves two pistols, a joker-wide smile
in the window of the flat iron building
at the center of the changing City / country.
no Emma Lazarus. Robert De Niro in Taxi Driver.
the statue of liberty on benzedrine.
the new New Colossus, a mother
of exiles, is not a jewish socialist.
Scorsese's american trope is Mailer's
white beat, the tired, disaffected cool
& latent rage of feeling
like you're owed something
you could never collect. a generation
trying to kick cold turkey the City/
country's broken promise, Rockwell's
false image, Hoover's chicken-in-every-pot.
but it's not just Norman's here: the children
of Chicana factory shifts form Mestiza punk
collectives that organize fiestas
for affordable housing rights; the illest
emcees Cliff Clavin by day & stalk
the mic at night in grey-blue tuxedo pants
they didn't have time to Clark Kent out of;
Howie's down the street slanging vinyl
at The Beat Parlor; Kendal's in the basement
providing access to herb & Black Nationalist Lit:
a mass of fiends stalk the six-way
looking for some sort of fix.

WELCOME TO WICKER PARK

is scrawled at the base of the poster
hurriedly on cardboard, as if to say:

you're still without home, this is temporary
as if to say: if you ended up here
something has gone   terribly wrong.

1994

A Portrait of the Artist in the Hood

the typewriter is from mt. sinai's resale shop

it is cool & all i can afford.

the writers i love are white boys
who love Black culture. hip-hop
put me here. in this chair
at the kitchen table. the blunt
in my hand. i'm smacked
trying to hold it all together.

the expressways were built
& my parents remember.
they left & i return.
an aliyah like my people before
to a populated land.

i was born here
but haven't been in some time.
my grandfather grew up a few blocks
from where i'm dizzy with smoke.

what does it mean when we appear

the children of white flight

back
    again

where am i supposed to be
where i am supposed to be
where am i supposed to be
where i am supposed to be

where am i supposed to be
where i am supposed to be
where am i supposed to be
where i am supposed to be
where am i supposed to be
where i am supposed to be
where am i supposed to be
where i am supposed to be
where am i supposed to be
where i am supposed to be

(what else would i write about)

WHiTE ON THE BLOCK

1

the first night was early august when even the eve refused to cool. it was past midnight. i asked the Kings outside if they knew where i could get something cold to drink. i could use a beer, a jug of water, something to keep me from being hot & lonely. i asked if they wanted anything, this group of four young men: skinny & Mexican & tattooed wearing white tank tops & jean shorts & bulls hats with silver necklaces, the makings of mustaches. they all just looked at me. i asked again & the street was actually quiet for once & the quiet stretched taut over the city like a wire around the neck. these boys didn't say shit, just looked at me, for fifteen seconds in silence that could've been an hour. the older looking of the four said there's a gas station on Ashland. i said thank you & started to head that way until under his breath he said they'd take a six=pack. his homies giggled. i looked back & laughed & the leader shot a look to the rest like *what's so funny.*

when i got back, we opened a case & sat on the stoop. they made the steps a school room. mapped out the neighborhood, block by block, who ran what streets. what beef. names. signs. colors. counts. bishops. conservative Vice Lords. peoples & folk. five & six point stars. almighty, insane. gang affiliates & factions. they were stuck here. moving white & weed. trapped in the trap. they could not leave without heat, a constant look over the shoulder.

2

i stroll anywhere
anytime. dayglow, moon
night. my skin
a pass. a piss
a joke, a way
out, always.
i stole, got caught
let go. no record

stalks me thru courtrooms.
i have no history
upon arrival. i am
always writing it.
i drink & drive
been pulled over
by CPD / nothing
thankfully. it's not luck
it's just / white. on the block
in the streets. the city's
mine. art institutes
collect my image.
i can tilt my fitted
toward any nation.
i'm a welcomed
guest. a warning shot.

my reputation precedes me.

JAYSON

dated Lena
a skinny girl from Ohio; i dated
Gina, her friend from undergrad.
naturally we moved in together
1632 W. Beach St., the beginning & first
apartment in Wicker. we worked
as waiters. covered each other's
shifts. i began writing in the morning
like religion. Jayson was trying to find
something to keep him alive.

his father photographed the famous
for *Ebony*. Black & middle-class
enough to move to Evanston.
his only older brother learned
multiplication, how a pack
becomes a brick & mortar
a laundromat front.

he took pics like his pops but the light
dim in his eyes. his brother amped
he moved to a neighborhood in transition
where a shoebox could become a wall
in the closet, bundles beneath the bed.
the carpet littered with tiny blue bags.
scales on the faux marble kitchen counter.

a giant diamond appeared in one ear.
a rope chain over his black tee.

i came home one night before he hit the club.
he left the restaurant weeks ago. there's a business
card sitting on the table, just his first name written
in cursive, beeper number at the bottom, beaming

like he is

the dopest   thing i've ever seen

D is our OTHER Roommate

a long boy, a tall jew. cro-magnon
with Samson's hair. he's quiet.
a giant who takes such little space.
a twin mattress on the floor in the tiny
third room. no dresser drawers.
clothes folded fastidious on the hardwood
like a gap employee in the fascism of retail.

an israeli army dissenter, who didn't
want to kill Palestinians & fled
after Rabin was murdered.

we drove a white truck
all over the city. picking up
& dropping off reupholstered sofas
from the Westside all the way to wilmette.
we lugged armoires up three flights
of rickety back steps, hanging over bannisters
hung over ourselves.

we learned the grid like marksmen.
a number; 1600 is Ashland, Western 2400
how blocks change cause of a letter: N to S
east to west.

all day we crossed viaducts. D playing
the radio, replaying the war;
border guards & second-class citizenship.
he was on the lam, dumbstruck.

MR. ROOSTER

grows tomatoes & jalapeños in the backyard.
he offers me mint & lime. his teeth wide as rows
of tombstones. drinks long-neck bottles of Tecate
from a red cooler planted on the porch. he roots
on the stoop & watches Beach St. litter with children.
in the lot across the way they play on a mattress
with an alley cat in the tall weeds sprouting dandelions
& purple-headed flowers. his round body posts beneath
the moon of a porch light, an indigenous king in baby blue
jeans & a dark denim jacket. when he returns from the third shift
at the butcher shop, he puts down his knife & washes the blood
from his hands. we know it's dawn when we hear the release
of air, the pop of the cap, the first sip as his friend strums
a small guitar & night creeps to sun & the sun rises like Jesus
or Jésus or poor Lazarus who mighta wanted to get some
rest or just stay right where he was. the block calls him
Mr. Rooster cuz he sings a Spanish blues, la melancolía
waking the neighborhood, announcing the new day.

THE LANDLORD

wears a phone on his belt
like a gun. each call so urgent
he must quick draw. he wears gold
sunglasses in the winter & cargo shorts
year round. his face a baby butt
rash from vacation in the Caribbean
or somewhere in Mexico though
collecting rent's the closest he's been
to Mexicans.

he lives in a suburb 20 minutes away
& works downtown. he owns four
other buildings in the neighborhood
& is buying more before the bubble
breaks or bottoms or tips over. he
& a college buddy have a side business
buying empty lots that might serve pork-
belly in a cafe with rusted candelabras.

he wears flip flops with socks
& wants to flip properties
like a wrestler. this rigged match.
this hollywood sport. this fantasy
economy anyone can pull up
their bootstraps. he talks to me
cuz i'm white like him & not
like my roommate or anyone else
he takes money from.

he steps out his BMW
onto the block like a petit prince
a conquistador. the only Spanish he knows
is *mañana es mia.*

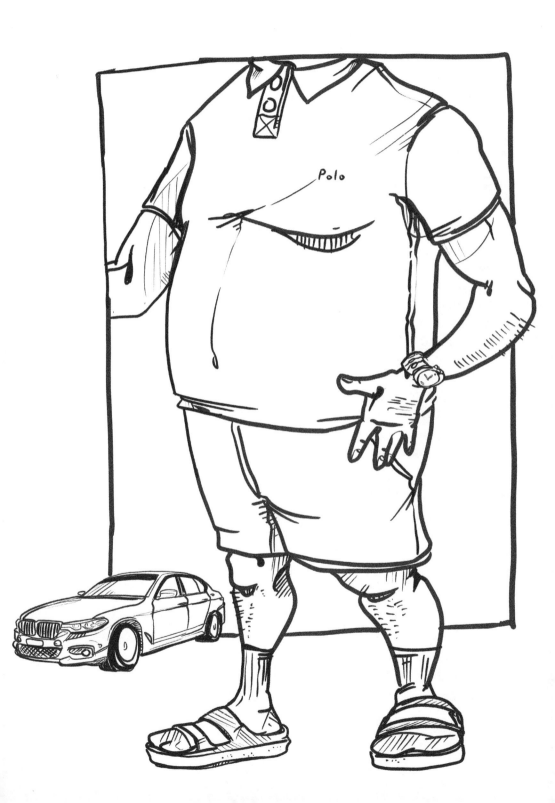

Boy Becomes Man

in the park. sips brass
monkey from a corner store
bought with a dollar & change.
he heard it in a beastie boys song.
his ID says he's old enough to drink
alone in the new city. it's near midnight
on a friday. the streets swell with folks
but the boy will not speak
to someone for days.

during days off
he'll watch. he'll lose
track of time. he'll learn
the city by listening to it
halt & grind & fire.
the boy will aspire
                    but for now
there is a corkscrew
unfurled in his hand
for the walk home.
his pocket got a knot in it.
tips scrambled for the little
he makes, he scrambles

scared someone will fuck with him.
scared no one will fuck with him.

the new city's burped
& birthed him, got him drunk
& taught him how to hold liquor.
how to piss in an alley.
how to run & cut
thru an alley.
how to open

someone's face
like a bottle of wine.

CAFE MATOU

The Chef

became lonesome for english & a good cheeseburger & returned to
american kitchens a sought-after star. opened his own spot at the end
of an empty Milwaukee Ave where Wicker's bohemian pack had not
yet come. new french cuisine in a small storefront for less than half of
what you'd pay in the bistros downtown. he ran the kitchen like a tyrant
improvising. steaks were high & seared in butter, a sprig of rosemary.
if you order the wrong dish or leave it in the window too long, a pot
might come for your head. his temper like the temperature.

an upstart venture on a mound of debt. some nefarious lenders, some
banks. both will kill you.

Chef would braise a pork chop like it was on fire. herb jus just the liquid
to save it. everyday he made an employee meal at 4:30 & we ate like a
family. after the night, he sat with a customer or alone at the end of the
bar with a glass of wine, still in his white coat, a soldier in fatigues after
battle. once in a while he'd apologize if the pan hit you but mostly he'd
just sit & sip & teach me how an artist works: relentless & with fury.

*

Amy the Manager's also a Buddha

waiting tables is learning how to juggle three or more hatchets at once.
the moment your attention's deterred the whole thing can go left. a busy
saturday night, its own rhythm. a couple of mistakes; the difference
between a livable wage & being late on the first. the service economy
dependent upon how a class or two above happens to feel. if i did 20
tables, i could leave with a baby knot. 5 shifts a week, i could cross the
poverty line.

Amy saw me struggle. flustered by the demands of a big party, my
mood soured by a pretentious two-top. she grabbed me mid-service as

i stumbled thru an evening, half the restaurant full & half my mind in
a notebook or some girl's bedroom or the hope of something more. her
hands firmly on my shoulders, face inches from mine, said *water waits for
no rock, it moves around & over. that's what water does. it flows. be water &
keep it pushing.*

*

Virgil the Sommelier

Queer as the cabaret he'd sing in on off nights. sometimes as himself,
sometimes as one of the women inside. there are multiple iterations of
everyone; G-d & grape. at the end of a night he'd sit me at the head
of the bar & lay multiple glasses, like Bozo buckets, on the freshly
wiped countertop. he'd grab bottles from dramatically lit shelves
twirling & telling stories about clubs, drugs & dick in the 80's: a foul-
mouthed show-girl. each glass a tiny taste; an entire evening dedicated
to Beaujolais, Bordeaux, Burgundy, another night solely of Sémillons.
Cognac's a variety of Brandy & i wanted to be down. he'd hold a glass
to the light, a quick swirl to show me its legs. tells me to put my nose all
the way into the bouquet, savor the liquid in the cup of my tongue. the
pallet expansive: floral & fruit, earth & pear there, wood & chocolate all
in a droplet. an ancient monastic alchemy of origin & grain.

Virgil, my fabulous professor, dancing Queen sommelier.

*

Leon

gives me a crash course in fine dining finishing school. how to delicately
place Coq au Vin on a guest's plate with fork & spoon then ladle au jus.
the order & swiftness of wine service; the proud, non-judgmental display
of the label, the gift of the cork to sniff at the base of the glass stem, the
tiny pour to taste & pleasure in pushing a whole bottle of Châteauneuf
du Pape. juggler of courses & plates. how to hold three dishes with
grace. four's a slop house. present the food on the red carpet of the white
table cloth with *je ne sais quoi.*

he makes more tips than i thought possible. one night over a thousand when a made man gave everyone in his vicinity a C-note. he'd count the night's take in an alcove near the side work, wrap his cash in a brown paper bag flat & tight & slides it in his waist band near a gun, a gold heart, a sick wife. the greatest server the city's ever seen.

*

Tony & Angela & then Angela

Tony would saturday night with a table of good fellas. steak au poivre & lamb on the bone. a few times he was in with his family. Angela's his girlfriend. there's no judgment in service. you bring someone what they desire. Tony's an investor & never paid for his meal but tipped well, especially when Angela was there. she'd inquire about dessert but rarely ordered. she liked the music we played & wondered at the artists. i asked if she knew Gang Starr or Guru or Donald Byrd or Roy Ayers. she said i should make her a mixtape. i told her i wasn't trying to get killed.

years later at the post office that's now a gym, i saw her ready for another set of lunges. i wanted to say hi, for her to recognize me like when i'd bring crème brulee to the table & her smile was a celluloid dream. eyes on burnt sugar then up at me, alight & alive, when i was glad to be a part of her day that was sweet.

*

The Guys in the Kitchen

are my age. Jose
the sous chef, takes the expressway

from Cicero, has 2 kids & a girl. Pele
washes dishes & lives around the way

wears a sleeve of names. hopes to move away.
his family came to make bank. america a way

post-nafta. we listened to crucial conflict, smoked hay
in the middle of the alley. they'd talk shit in Spanish, wey

the rhythm & play of the ball court. after a tough shift, a way
to bust out laughing. my Spanish broke as me, wey.

didn't know what they meant, each sentence punctuated, wey.
i thought maybe i heard an additional syllable, YHWH

my G-d, these dudes save me some nights, affirm my way.
from buey, literally an ox, a labor & sacrifice, a razor blade

Big L told us. we cut up thru the evening, pool tips con hombres
count bills in the back, we scrape, to get by, any fucking way.

THE JOBS

the barkeep.
the milkmaid.
the pierogi molder.
the sweatshop sewer.
the steel worker.
the automated lever
       everyday
       for thirty years.
the furniture seller.
the kolache baker.
the concha baker.
the butcher.
the supermercado bagger.
the paletero.
the fruit cart slicer.
the tajín sprinkler.
the steel worker.
the automated lever
       when factories left
       no one could afford to eat
       at the taqueria, the polish diner.
the ingenuitous pimps.
the street walkers.
the corner kids
       moving white.
the white flight.
the hood of hustlers
       overnight.
the divestment.
the abandoned carcass.
the real estate vultures.
the steam punk squatters.
the drug den denizens.
the artist studios.

the coffee shop.
the thrift shop.
the storefront gallery.
the used bookstore.
the new restaurant with
the tattooed chef.
the music venue.
the barback.
the bar's back.
the art's here.
the art's for sale.
the SROs
the single family homes.
the night life.
the knife fight.
the guns patrol
       where guns patrolled.
       where five years ago
the new homeowners
       wouldn't go.
       it's seedy
       then unique.
the boutique.
the urban outfits.
the cute developments.
the real estate loan officers.
the offices & officers.
the internet tech startups.
the flat iron.
the artist loft office space.
the sweatshops.
the whole floor.
the whole foods.
the strip malls that made suburbia.
the jobs that made the hood
       obsolete like
the iceman
       cold in this new economy.

SAVIORS of EL BARRIO

iron hands the color of oil.
blue shirts stained like church
glass. the young guys still got fresh
lines from the barber. old heads let it
go a little. all the fellas at the tire shop
know how to submerge rubber in a bath
to determine what caused rupture.
detectives of the tread under broke
fluorescent suns, a forest of dead
Michelin men. source of constant rescue.
roadside assistance for the hood
long after the sign says closed.
community festival notices taped
in the window. styrofoam coffee cups
filled with filth. an empty bottle
of henny is a good saturday night.
black shoes & black belts of the lug
wrench. sockets spin out of hubcaps
like a dice game. yellow jacks lift
cars on the corner, hercules
with a seesaw. some wear back
braces. most have tattoos, gold
crosses around their necks, down
to save anyone who pulls up.

URBiS ORBiS

Urbis Orbis will always be a haven
for those of us who don't have a home
in this country, this society, this city.

Tom, the owner

the center of bohemia. a giant room
machines once lived. shut down
moved on. an all-day seat costs a buck 80.
Tom the owner used to shoot
i heard. grew up in the suburb next
to mine. now sits in the middle of an oval
bar chatting quietly with regulars
reading newspapers & Derrida. white
mugs turn beige. Brown neighborhoods
turn white. during the day, light leaks
over chess games like piss. people & tables
scatter like buck shot. no baristas. the difference
between those who work & those who hang out
indiscernible. you pour your own refills.
shady shit always seems to be happening:
the night i meet Rudy & Alonzo we cop
a bag out the alley after they ask if i'm
a cop. David the sculptor takes me around
the corner to his studio. shows me a gun
& asks if i'll act a look-out for a liquor store
hold up. the girl India's eyes are an ocean
after the Exxon. her room, a palace of sadness.
Larry's got locks. 13 years sober trying to raise
his daughter right. the light at night made
our bullshit ethereal. all of us leads in a low
budget film that'll never get made.
we gather here seeking a home
we'd never name, some book never
published, some painting tucked in

a closet, closed up, gone. grown. some
away forever. some regular life.

it's a gym now.
monthly fees.
members only.

RUDY

was a sailor. two tours in the first gulf war.
a castoff. after we met, i saw him everywhere.
he's well-loved on Milwaukee Avenue
& seems to work at half the restaurants.
he could get anything you ever wanted: opium
a pocketknife, spray paint. he always had a girl
a thin dark-haired beauty, new to the city
small dog in tow. he'd end up crashing with her
a few weeks in some loft with marble countertops
& after they fought & broke, he'd hit the block
like a summer jam. he'd paint canvases
of flowers he saw in Iraq; clusters of bellflower
bunches of yellow chamomile. he'd drop acid
& skateboard downtown, unanchored, well past
business hours when buildings would flower
like bombs in the sky. it was a time
when no one had a last name
only their first followed by a brief description:
Rudy who works at Earwax.
Rudy with the ponytail.
Rudy with eyes like whirlpools.
Rudy with tattoos of violets.
Rudy who skateboards.
Rudy with the PTSD.
Rudy who said to meet him here.
Rudy who said i could stay with you.
Rudy who owes me forty bucks.
you know Rudy, the sailor
the painter, the busboy
the veteran, ghost addict.
Rudy the con artist
the hook up, the petty thief
& personal chef to the homeless.
Rudy the hero of Milwaukee Avenue.
my first friend in the new city.

EARWAX

a gentrified pastoral ending on a Shakespearean remix

light trapped in the storefront. door ajar to the avenue.
dust dancing an errant sun beam. the must of espresso
& pesto mingles with new money buying mansions
lining the park. white aprons, oil stained tassels. hairnets

on the heads of young men being moved out
the neighborhood. vintage seats, repurposed school
desks. Big Star, the white taco spot, still a car wash.
a menagerie of lamps, a vegan haven. freak show

posters, posers, all day diners. carnies selling a dream
& hashish. frog-legged boys & beards. men dwarfed
by history. six-fingered guitar strummers. everyone
an indie-band, wondrous skeleton & snake charmer.

tattooed women pass an hour with Huxley; *how
many hideous / beauteous creatures in this brave new world.*

1108 N. Hermitage

an apartment of poems (too broke for a suite)

B

i mis-gendered him
at first, a whole generation
of Chicago boys who grew up
in House, comfy with a spectrum
of style & sexuality.

his uniform: silver booty shorts
roller skates & high white socks
with candy cane stripes, a mesh
tank top. he wears beads of sweat
like jewels, a camera or two
like medallions.

B's at every party. every night
there's a DJ & dance floor to praise.
he pops out, pops a shot & whispers
into the ears of all the women
i thought too beautiful to talk to.
every time he conjures a smile
a magician, as they hid hair behind
an ear to offer the fruit of their lobe.

eventually we speak. he tells me
he's at work on a pictorial document
of the scene. its glory & horror. its ecstasy
& heavy drugs. jack & juke journalism.

he says i should come to dinner.

★

Melody

is B's girl.

a wisp of a woman from southern illinois.
wheat thin & virginia slims. hair a haystack.
the freckles of a farm girl. her breasts a bounty
a bowl of blood oranges. she spoke in a 50's twang
Rizzo-esque. there's a hard edge, a chronic hint
at past distress. her dress, a lyrca halter. she looks
18 but feels forever like her youth evaporated an era
before she was born.

they live in the attic turned loft. a long run
of a room with pillows on the floor to sit, low
tables, enough fabric for a Moroccan gift shop.
they sleep atop a bunk bed. there are bowls
of salad & plates of hummus & olives. hash
rolled in spliffs. acid jazz & breakbeat science.
candles & the leaking light of street lamps. Laurel
the downstairs neighbor is there.

*

Laurel

has a lazy eye. close cropped
bone blonde hair. a tattoo on her scalp
of a black rose. Laurel's an adjunct professor
at columbia college. Laurel makes pictures
of dead things & ghosts: skulls on a dinner table
tricks of light that look like the faces of ancestors.
i'm not smart enough to understand. Laurel
teaches me to say *make* pictures. *take* is patriarchal
make implies the hand of a creator, a conversation
& manipulation of vision, a reframing. Laurel's
the first person i know to have her own apartment.
art on the walls from colleagues, paintings of past lovers.
she's a decade older & i'm a cave man recent

to language. she makes me feel all broad back,
bone & stamina. Laurel has a room dedicated to sex.
equipment like a gym class. a whole weekend in her
house of lavender. i'm a brute learning not to crush
a bird, a dumb man just beginning to speak.

★

Geoff & Alexa

also live in the building. she's from
cambridge, wealthy, beautiful & unemployed.
Geoff's in a phd program at the university
of chicago studying postmodern philosophy
writing about Derrida & deconstruction.
their apartment's wallpapered in aluminum.

Alexa djs industrial techno
not the soulful elevation of what Chicago
& B dig but the early electro iterations
of what happened in the abandoned houses
of Detroit steel. iron symphonies of a tweaker
in the war on drugs, in the moment industry
fled the heartland to leave space for the sonic
experimentations of the first generation of kids
who would make less than their parents.

Geoff & Alexa take me to Crobar, a club
i could never afford. Alexa knows the bartender
the coat room girl, the guys at the door. a princess
of the night with tiny bags of candy. Geoff follows
& puts a pill in my mouth. the space is a monstrosity
multiple rooms & walls of music, stories of speakers
lights low & throbbing. models, investment bankers
& basketball players souped up on designer drugs.
MDMA disorientation. house distorted, a night train

quickly gentrifying, white like the powders, white
like the peoples.

*

Crazy Horse

Melody asks if i'll take her
to the interview. she's the type
not many say no to. i drive
an '84 volkswagen rabbit
i bought off my cousin for a g
when i turned 16. it's a rag
top. we hit North Ave like Thelma
& Louise dipped in denim & a sundress.

The Crazy Horse is a gentleman's club.
today is Melody's audition. she has
to dance & sweet talk. she takes a bump
in the car before we go in. she worked
in Rockford & Joliet but this is a shot
at real bread. her homegirl says $1200
a week, at least.

the spot's swank, a grotto of purple
mirrors & warm neon. the waitresses
look like they swing from serving
to the stage. Melody says i can watch
her interview if i wish. i'm a gentleman
so i wait outside the back office
standing at attention like a soldier
a Kevin Costner, guard of import
my body a tool of use & value.

*

the end of sociology

Melody comes to the crib to ask what she says is a big favor.

a phd student's writing his dissertation & wants to spend 24 hours
in the lives of his subjects immersed in
the work. there's a little bit
of bread & will i spend the night
cuz she don't know dude & B's out of town.

of course i'm down

the professor takes us to dinner anywhere she wishes.
Melody never had sushi & a spot just opened on Division.
the waitress brings towels before the meal to wash.
the professor orders sake & maki & asks Melody
about her life, her parents & education. he records
on tape how her moms would leave in search
of a man, her absent father, Melody's on some
teen wonder woman shit, sacrificed herself so her siblings
could glimpse normal. her dyslexia undiagnosed.
she dropped out of school & waitressed as a sophomore.

started dancing at 18 cuz there was more money to be made
& g-d gave me these titties for a reason, she said. she's paying
for her sister's college, for real, in her first year at Eastern.

it's hard not to fall in love.

the professor says you eat the ginger
after the meal. but we keep putting
the little slivers of spicy flesh on top
of the fish. we like mixing everything up.

we go to a dive after & the professor
makes the mistake of trying to match shots
with us. we know the bartender & the street
& how to hold liquor. the professor gets shit-
faced & we bring him back to the apartment
to sleep it off.

Melody makes a fortress of pillows
& sheets in the middle of the long room.
she plays The Ramones & The Clash & rolls
a spliff. we stretch into night & she talks
about Chicago & leaving & returning with more
money & fame. we fall asleep for a little & i wake
with her head on my chest. i kiss her temple
awake. she raises her mouth to mine
                                    & we jump.

*

everyone ghosts

i never see anyone again. after that night
Melody & i know better. the house broke
& primarily drug related. i was thinking
about doing less anyway, felt i was relying
too tough on something other than myself.

plus she's not trying to leave B

                              but maybe

a year later, i see her
in a big baby
blue Olds with bench seats.
she's out. moving west.
like vegas, west, all her shit
in the back seat.

she's flying solo.
she doesn't get out of the car.
i just lean into her
window for a little
saying my goodbyes
softly, out
          on the Ave.

RAVE

when the internet was a flyer
        someone put in your hand
a word from a mouth near enough
        to whisper. there's a number
to call, a fake address to send you
        off. a forgotten warehouse
where the party jumped . . .

we didn't have to go thru the rigmarole.
we knew Rye-kn; a free-wheeling, up & coming
drum & bass selector, who always knew
where to get the good shit.

                              *drum & bass:
                    the Caribbean churned thru the raw mouth
                of post-industrial, post-colonial mad max car speakers,
            triumphant sped-up dub platters & Method Man's chopped
            vocals sprinkled like glass shards; a music for the end times.

Danny the Wild Child
went from backyard parties
to top-billin. records dug
in bridgeport thrifts
& George's Music Room.
a White Sox cap on his head
like a Southside king.

when molly was ecstasy
        unstepped on mdma
& the come down
        no ground tooth lockjaw.
euphoric & bullshit. all we'd need:
        a moon & a warm body.
Chicago was
        the murder capital, for real.

its children lug milk
           crates into reclaimed public
space the private corporate state
           owns. on the day they tried to kill
our parents' jobs

we were flying
you couldn't find us

Millie was the belle
of the ball. she came home
the first night we met, naked
under a new street lamp on Beach St.
but never returned. i insisted
on a condom when the whole scene's
who you could trust. a small pocket
of people & pills. we were
in a storage facility
while the guard slept;
third generation jackers
new skool tweakers
off the shits, grinding
til the change
of the base drop
& shift.

tHE BoP SHoP

i was there when liquid kitty used to be The Bop Shop

—J.U.I.C.E.

jazz embraced its son.
old heads in Kangols
recognize the snot-nosed
foul-mouthed motherfuckers
in oversized denim. a Tuesday
work night to put in work.
when a freestyle was off the dome
in the tradition of the city's great
improvisers; Phil Cochran & Viola Spolin.

glasses sweat like the crowd
gathered in layers before the band
stand; hoodied monks, strong heads
nod in approval, a ritual to keep
the crowd moving. young bucks might
fuck up which meant heads would stop
& you could get stomped but homeboy
could return next week after practice.
rap's gymnastics, kids flipping in empty lots
on a mattress, an art & kung-fu dance.
when emcees were swordsmen
who carried words in a velvet case
& polished brass when they'd get to the bar.
all day long, a generation mumbling
to themselves over the rumble of L trains.
mad men superheroes who hold down day
jobs & emerge in the night with bombastic
nome-de-plumes: Shadow Master, Eyespy
Longshot, J.U.I.C.E., Ang 13, Prime, Captial D.

Tuesday's a proving ground, wordshop
workshop, masterclass, shogun swap meet
spot to see new poets from sides of the city
the city didn't want you to see.

we were out there, on Division
catching wreck & getting open.

Lit - X

ending on a remix of Howl

underground saturday night
in the basement of the six-way.
steps down to the bookstore.
incense, drums, prayers. Black
& mostly that. poems, a song.
a gathering, a cipher. communal
healing. here would be the start
of my life unconstrained
by northside segregationists.
a life of Black poems i'd been
preparing for. reading alone.
here they were for real. i am
& always will be that white
dude. another one & yet again.
the trope of the culture. will i be
different if the country isn't.
on the side, then on the mic
in the center, yet again.
here is the beginning. the X
marking the spot i was born
again. in / to / out / of the caldron
Mario, Tina Howell, Chuck Perkins
Reggie Gibson seasoned. here
where i met avery r. young
Dennis Kim & Brother Mike.
where i saw the freshest minds
of my generation employ bad
assness, stark lyrical aching
bragging themselves Black
into the streets til dawn.

Denizen

the only way i know a song
knocks is to play it in your truck;
a ford big enough to explore rap
dreams, seemingly attainable
in the cabin of our cruise ship.

first generation Korean-american.
your little brother also an emcee
& still alive. the GOAT
poet / rapper in the history
—of the hybrid.

we went to rival high schools
but met in the basement
of Lit-X; earnest kids with spiral notebooks
& jeans two sizes too big, trying to get on
& a word in edgewise.

you rap for your people
born with two tongues, Typical Cats
regular joes, immigrant stories
Chicago / america is reticent to claim.
your sing-song style bread
crumbs the generation now
gathers in the crates
of an old oak, a cd stuck
in their parent's dodge. a budding
pidgin. to think your folks wanted
you to be an architect. the whole time
you were the blueprint.
                              all summer
your truck bumped All-City.
we'd pull up, pop out; hit the corner
store, hoops court, park jam, bbq;

a constant movie; a moving cipher
weed rolled, we'd roll, nowhere to go.
windows down, before the fall, before
you said the ancestors stopped
whispering to you like that & the Last
Child was working on a record
& all of us were still alive.

ANNA ♡

looks at me once & it feels like all night.
she's Jeremy's girl. Jeremy works with Jayson
& i at Wildfire. he's every emo indie guitar player.
she's the daughter of a Filipina nurse & an eastern european
house painter. she dons a platinum-blonde wig & long eyelashes
fake as fuck. smokes parliament thins & plays stand-up bass
in an all-girl ska band. she lives on the top floor west
of Western in the tallest building on North Ave
the living room is for band rehearsal. she serves
champagne & Hennessey in mason jars. i see her
around at house parties. we go to a rave on Webster
hop a fence & cross the old bridge to get there.
we make out beneath a billboard & spend the summer
falling asleep to Sea & Cake. she's bipolar & pansexual.
wears a kimono open with panties around the long apartment
at any hour regardless of who's there. she don't care or hide.
she's high. a fine mess of a woman & i love a good mess.
a long cigarette dangling like a delicate fruit at the stove
making eggs. tummy, ass & eggs. last night's mascara
smeared about her eyes like perfect wafts of smoke.

WE WERE JUST A PHASE

on the day the landlord raised the rent
25%   (which we thought illegal
                       but what lawyers did we know
                       what loot could we wrangle)
i had a duffle bag of clothes
a typewriter i carried like a briefcase
an '88 chevy nova that was a library.

i'd see Jayson one more time
departing Old Town Ale House
on North smiling like the skyline.
he was out, had a man, retired
from the game of bundles & closets.
we shook up on the Ave. he took a dollar
out his pocket, tore it in two & told me
to hold half. i keep it in my wallet, still, today.
we said we'd stay in tune but it's hard in a city
of rush streets & tumble.

D had an army-issued backpack
slung across his chest.

he walked to the train
without goodbye
& disappeared into the subway's
sunken stomach

tHE TiME I WAS HoMELESS & tHE CAR WAS AlSO A BANK

at least the diners stay open
late: the ham-on-bone at Western,
the long car on Irving, the white
palace at Roosevelt; temples
of halogen lights & refillable mugs
where waitresses are kind
& sometimes the hand
they put to mine to lift
my head from nodding
is the only time i'm touched
that day.

i know where homes is
tucked beneath the kennedy.

i've known the north branch
of the Chicago River at dawn
long before i signed a lease.
bags of clothes. books. a city
-wide storage locker, the only
key in my pocket. i sleep
in my car, i sleep at my mans
my mentors, my girl's
before i lose her.

2 a.m. couch surfer. sucker.
baked bean aldi booster.

the tips i take
at the end of my own shift
are rolled in a bustelo can
tucked in the space
the spare's supposed to be

next to a knife, a roll
of quarters, a quart of
Listerine, a bar of Irish
Spring, a tooth
brush, a box cutter.

i do laundry at the Y.
i'll clean anyone's clock.

ODE TO THE WAITRESS

egalitarian nurse. 20% psychologist. you cure
our ailments for an hour or whatever, under
any light / night / joint / condition you find us.
it's like you took a Hippocratic oath to kindness
despite our thristy advances you cut down
like a lumberjack. despite the wage gap.
mood wed to income. incomparable actress
who brings me & my head-ass homies eggs at 3 a.m.
with the grace of a film star in color-vision.
we all feel lovely when you call us *honey*. it's not
that i can be whoever i wish in front of you
but i can be myself finally without shame.
high priestess of the Golden Nugget who bore
extra napkins the morning my aunt passed.
temptress of the BBQ who touched my shoulder
when dropping the tab, who loved me for a month
& dropped me like the tab. you are all good
to my father who holds your hand every time
for too long & i tell him to stop but get shooed away
cuz this is lite work in a heavy lift & maybe a moment
to catch your breath in the whirlwind of the weeds.
you are a beautiful breed. excuse us all. who sees
who serves the people more, our needs & insane
demands, our idiot-synchronicities. who is more
resilient than a mature dervish wheeling side dishes
& heaping pots. ballerina of the four top. you take us
in & return us to the world fuller then when we came.

ODE TO 22's IN A BROWN PAPER BAG

drinking outside's the freest
we could possibly be. everyone
wishes to walk in the stew
of summer clutching a canteen filled
with cold gas as night sweats
the base of your back, gathering
tiny pools underarm like little
armies of funk. forget the law
which governs state agencies. this
the law of close quarters in concrete.
a necessity of sharing a bedroom
or two with someone stressing you
after the gig or kids turnt up on television
& kool aid. the thick of glass in a bag
in your fist down the street, slinking
thru a park like an animal unseen
around these parts for quite some time.
a free being recently departed from a dollar
& some change is dangerous, lives as if
anything's possible.

THE 6·WAY on the SABBATH

The Sabbath was made for man, not man for the Sabbath

Mark 2:27

every friday after sundown
a ten-block walk to the intersection at Damen.
we won't stop in the liquor store or scrounge
change for an elote. we won't turn on lights
or spend a dollar. we quick step past section 8
lots gut bare. no trespassing. if time's abundant
a slink thru side streets to see scribbles of madmen.
most often a devout hustle down North Ave
to consecrate the corner & get a spot in the minyan
with men posted up at the 6-way intersection.
a mechitza, a partition between us & those
we won't see on a tuesday. we're a motley flock
invisible to the newly paid. our cessation
from work lasts till the first three stars emerge
in the Westside sky or some other miracle: a 20
falling out a pocket like a lost feather, a bag
of bottles left too long unattended, a truck bed
open for the quick take. our incessant con
to get over & get by.

G-d could rest after day six.
we scramble thru all seven.

All the Men on the Ave

all the men on the ave
keep one foot on the wall
& one in the earth. Black
flamingos posted like capital
P's. David, Jeff, Oba. no one
has an address or last name.

all the men on the ave
jaundice-eyed & fire-tongued.
mad dog breath. bare bottles
are bells at their feet. offerings
to an Orisha left back South
side.

all the men on the ave
got grocery carts of metal.
Latino / Polish workers
on new construction sites
turn their kind eyes elsewhere
leave out copper fragments
in this new economy of not.

all the men on the ave
know the alleys are treasure
maps. haul other men's trash
to the recycling center on North.
trade their weight for a few bucks
a few bucks for a bottle or some
other triumph at day's end
before night scrambles to sleep
if sleep at all.

all the men on the ave
dress in gowns of gladiators

from smaller markets
where jobs flew
like southern game.

all the men on the ave
are a team   of superstars
who want the rock & won't pass
hopefully   thru the chronic night.

all the men on the ave
are awake, painfully.
lights hanging overhead
in place of the heavens.

OBA

carries photocopies
the Korean owner lets him make
for free. he's got originals too
tucked in a cabinet, a beautifully
handwritten folder. Oba adds
to the stack daily. fires off
hundreds & hits the ave slanging
words all day long. each day a new song.
they go for a dollar. some he gives away.
he's generous that way. knows how to finesse
how to conversate. psychologist-comedian-
guru. street hyphenate; he's got poems
for days. poems about the new age
& the new folk comin.

Jeff Zimmerman paints a giant mural
of his face in an alley off Lake & Damen.
the mural gets blocked by new construction
but his eyes become the moon.
eyes cat-green & yellowed
eyes that welcome all who stroll by.
eyes trustworthy & necessary. & that's all
i expect from art, something to believe in
to have a function & serve it. the antithesis
of so much of the bullshit hanging in galleries
popping up along the ave.

eyes that stay   peeking into the future.

one night Oba puts a band together
at *Yo Mama's Cafe*. he plays the sax
& reads. baristas, bartenders & beer
backs come. musicians too. folks i hear
on the street or corner or late night at Estelle's;
a man the people know.

he knows & yells my name
from a half block away.
i always pay my dollar.
it's street tax. a luxury tuition
to study at the feet of Oba Maja
poet laureate of Milwaukee Avenue.

THE GALLERIST

squats in a storefront long enough to open a coffee shop / gallery
called *Yo Mama's Cafe*. he stretches the sun up in a doorway
on the avenue. the ancients wake & walk past. he's shirtless
in karate pants. lumberjack shirt, denim overalls & roller skates.
tremendous locks race down his back. he shaves his head
& wears snow goggles. in the summer he runs to the Arab
store for drum & rolling papers. there's an espresso constantly
steaming at his elbow. a canary. he carries hardbound books
in a belt strapped to his bicycle. Foucault & Public Enemy. Fear
of a Black Planet un-ejectable from his walkman. he's always
alone in thunderous headphones & has a hundred girls in his pocket.
his bed lays in the middle of a furniture-less future. he stirs a pot
of gumbo beneath the blue line & sells paintings he found in the alley
embellished with crowns. he's avenue royalty in a gas station onesie
chuck taylors jackson pollacked & laceless. he's 36 & a visionary.
he's 49 & a screwball. he's from the south. he is from the south
side. he's skateboarding down the ave in adidas joggers & a gas mask
three stripes & apocalypse, going nowhere in particular.

THIGAHMAHJiGGEE

we have the tallest buildings in the world here,
damn near, right? we are something, something
you shouldn't take lightly, take us serious.

Thigahmahjiggee aka Skarkula

got kicked out of circuit city
for dubbing tapes to sell.
you like hip-hop music
dressing all over your salad.
Maxwell St. mixtape hawker.
warm bear hugger. hunger.
train car sleeper with a contaminating grin.
beard Buddha, the happy one with arms
in the air. he just don't care. Martin Luther King
Jr. Whopper With Cheese. that free
associative. associates. hood famous
with david letterman aspirations.
aspergers. calamari astronaut.
tether-less in the era of kinkos.
he outlasted the chain
& the burger king
& the real world
& yuppie capitalism.
he delivers more than the tribune.
the only constant.
always on the hustle
five-dollar hollers.
Sharkula, will die
if he ever stops
moving.

DAViD

speaks in riddles. carries a harmonica
& a paper cup though he really wants
a brown bag filled with lightning. he says
his brother has a home for him in evanston
if he could make it there. his beard has grey
& he has seizures & one winter sleeps
in an empty school bus beneath the blue line
as hundreds of condos rise like an armada.
one night it's so cold he asks if he could sleep
in my apartment. it's the only thing he ever asks
of me. that & if i know where his brother hides
the key. he turns on & off every light switch
to control when the darkness returns.
he soaks in the tub for hours. harmonica on the edge
like a bar of soap. his nude body propped up.
streaks from the street lamp drape him
like an illuminated blanket. he eats an orange
& lets the peel cascade into the water like petals.

tHE OiL & INCENSE MAN

slangs scents so the public stays fresh.
he's got Malcolm's paperback in one pocket.
an accountant's ledger in the other. a light
blue button up beneath a khaki trench coat.
you smell him from three blocks away.
a forest of sticks lit & burning. a smoke stack
portable salesman able to skate if the cops come.
rambo ammo holsters X-ed across his chest:
amber, frankincense, & myrrh. the wise man
who woulda brought baby Jesus gifts & brings
holy odors to Jesus's mother off 26th.
kufi-ed & righteously perfumed off a red line
near you. a mobile economic plan. pink wands
wafting from a card table in a park. anointing
the neck with a bouquet of jasmine, nag champa
burnt offerings out a knapsack, a moveable feast
of sandalwood, permitless, & perpetually illegal.

1037 N. DAMEN

Mikey & i inherited the apartment from Anna
who lived there with Leo & made the baby Anton
& moved back to Baton Rouge to be with her people.

four bedrooms on the top floor of a three-story greystone.
Mikey's room, an earlobe down to Damen Ave we'd sit
on the stoop & drink on the weekends & watch the whole

hood whiten. Aunt Joyce is alive & says *weekends
are for amateurs* so we play cards, too broke to go out anyway
& project super mario brothers life-size on the living room wall.

we get high & have girls over & homies would yell up
to Mikey's room at 3 a.m. to see what was poppin after
the bars shuttered. Idris moved in after he & Krista broke

right before he met Felicia who he married. they made
the baby Taos & moved to New Mexico to be with her people.
but before we are a community center flop house hotel cathedral.

squad deep. there's Kristin, Tina, Lisa & names i didn't know.
Mikey met Cindy up the street at a party. she lives two doors
down at Augusta. he writes her a note & sticks it on the door.

they go on a date. she sleeps over & is loud in the night.
they move to Germany, get married & live in washington
state now. he writes poems & keeps in touch, mostly with Nate.

Nate'll go to school in Tennessee, then Michigan & i have no friends
again. every morning the last fall we live here, i take the blue line
& walk thru the apple-crisp air, right by 1750 W. Haddon

where George moved 100 years before. my life revolves around
one place, one apartment for a century. this city has no memory
only my own & i can't afford to stay. all my people are moving

all my people are memory & i'm right here, still alone, trying
to carve a community out of ghosts & the gone, trying to hang
on, weeping in the doorway, calling my ancestors' names.

How I met Idris (the Remix)

when a girl you know says
i have another friend who likes hip-hop
you think dude prolly corny
for no good reason except masculinity
a toxin & you on guard for wackness
like a vampire killer, in the era hip-hop's underground
at war with the empire & moving to strip malls
& pop charts. & true, no one knighted you a lancelot
for the culture but strictly hard-core heads ward off
clown-ass mugs like the plague.

        but she is your homegirl
after all & there's a house party
prolly for her bornday & our mans
Itch 13 is spinning records at the crib
which is live, not acid-in-the-punch live
tho the shit's mos definitely spiked.

the Black Frank white is alive
via Itch's hands, the first time he utters *Uh*
the apple bottom of the record funk drops
the spot. the whole body bounces up
by the second *Uh* & dudes *is mad*
i get more butt than ashtrays, my head raised
for the first time that night, scouring the room
for anyone to cosign the joyousness
the DJ, Craig Mack & especially
the heavy-breathed poet Christopher Wallace
animated east coast stomping, mean-mugging
the country, brings our modest saturday night turn-up

& sure enough, i see this other dude's
eyes recognize in the living room, in a sea
of heads bent, another head popped up

at the signal, same nod, same bat channel.
we prolly mouthed the whole verse
when most rappers we knew
& B.I.G. were still breathing
& we were

      young enough

            to be
gathering brothers, *everlasting*
like the toe on pro-keds.

                              R.I.P. Craig Mack

Jack × Juicy

rumor is

two lovers ride a tandem bike past 2 a.m.
when bars close to sketch until sun up:

billboards peeling like birchwood bloom Krylon colors;
doorframes that lead to dead apartments bear the dynamic duo's
signature;

Jack × Juicy

a tavern that stopped serving drinks long ago, it's widow eyes shuttered
lumps of coal, brighten again. their names separate

Jack × Juicy

but close enough to intimate the possibility
they held hands while doing it.

Jack × Juicy

a couple of bandit   lovers
wearing dawn as a cloak to paint stars on dead steel

& bring a neighborhood of foreclosed
storefronts back to life with gloriously free fonts.

Jack × Juicy

live here, love here
& remake the streets into a gallery

for all the people to see
admission always free.

A GiRL FROM tHE NEIGHBORHOOD

i asked my man to ask your girl for your number & bam we got 22s of
Honey Brown & walked the park. you said you wanted to hear something
i wrote. i whispered a little rap in your ear, beneath a giant oak

met you at the gig; an after-school arts program Vero dragged you to.
her husband rhymed & we worked together. you came to the settlement
house on Augusta in the sweaty-ass air of August. hair pulled back slick.
said some funny shit 'bout the food & smiled. said you wrote a bit too &
why that some sweet spot you put your palm to.

when i said *i'll pick you up at 7*, you thought i meant 8. i was on whiteboy
time. had to wait a half hour while you got ready & your not-really-
little-cousin Carlos baby giant full of slick talk & jibaritos, started to
roast me on the wooden stairs i came to know your uncle built.

Carlos bust out & said *yo you look like that dude from honey i shrunk the kids* &
the little ones cracked rainbow-colored smiles from freeze pops melting in
their hands & Carlos was victorious & not yet 11. later you told me his dad
was killed a year ago, a few blocks from where we stood.

the sun sunk west & all the apartments spread shadows on the ground
slow like a sheet unfurled in the few lovely moments it's suspended
above the earth, the bed, your body before finally falling.

we made it out on Milwaukee, walking south & stopped in front of
Earwax; the coffee shop i knew all the busboys & could g weed at. you
looked inside. said you weren't hungry. said you didn't eat white people
food, got mad at the idea of a veggie burger. all the new faces, all the
white faces, my own

in the glass. your eyes, Wells like the school, close. the lake, great,
ocean, crossing, bacalao & African bloodline. you said you couldn't go
there. this space wasn't for you. wondered what we were doing here.

a year & a half later we'd yell in the vestibule. you'd rip my shirt & the plastic buttons bounced down the steps your uncle built. & of course you were right.

but i'd hoped this was something different or i was or this was the city big enough to love you in.

ODE TO THE DIVE BAR

the long, drunk room a darkened sanctuary.
windows blocked opaque to make day insignificant
light impaired. in here's timeless. a deprivation
tank to meditate when the sky falls & you need
to revel in pissy swill & the certain stench
of someone else's body. in here's all better.
99 problems & a bottle of beer
on the wall. the condensation from whiskey
on the rocks is holy water when applied right.
a pit stop vacation from the day
for those who could never afford one.
a hades between work & the work of home.
a bridge to the well & wet ring a glass makes.
there's a myriad of reasons you might be mourning
here. there's a popcorn machine, a bag of Ruffles
a jukebox willing to suck your dirty bills for a little
bit of funk. the spot peeks at you out a side street.
its Old Style neon in the window winks, nods
to your anonymity. even a regular can disappear
here on the round & spin of a stool, beneath
a thousand thighs rubbed on the low; skirts, junk
touched in jeans, hips smashed against the evergreen
of a pool table. who hid night in a bottle. here
people know your name & forget it & shout it
in anger & elation. so much has spilled & i've spilled
so much & spilled onto a seat that saved me
on the occasion i needed to spill into someone.
respite or retreat, here's fellowship, a seat
reserved any day of the week. this thanks
giving family of strangers, ancient hall brimming
with inebriated comrades, a cheers to you:

our glasses raised & empty.

THE LONG DRUNK ROOM A DARKENED SANCTUARY WINDOWS BLOCKED OPAQUE TO MAKE DAY INSIGNIFICANT LIGHT IMPAIRED. IN HERE'S TIMELESS. A DEPRIVATION TANK TO MEDITATE WHEN THE SKYFALLS & YOU NEED TO REVEL IN PISSY SWILL & THE CERTAIN STENCH OF SOMEONE 99 PROBLEMS & ON THE WALL. THE ON THE ROCK A PIT STOP VACA

PURE GENUINE Old Style

THE SPOT PEAKS AT YOU OUT A SIDE STREET. ITS OLD STYLE NEON IN THE WINDOW WINKS, NODS TO YOUR ANONYMITY. EVEN A REGULAR CAN DISAPPEAR HERE ON THE ROUND & SPIN OF A STOOL, BENEATH A THOUSAND THIGHS RUBBED ON THE LOW; SKIRTS.JUNK TOUCHED IN JEANS. HIPS SMASHED AGAINST THE EVER GREEN POOL TABLE WHO HID NIGHT IN A BOTTLE. HERE PEOPLE KNOW YOUR NAME & FORGET IT & SHOUT IT IN ANGER & ELATION. SO MUCH HAS SPILLED & I'VE SPILLED SO MUCH & SPILLED ONTO A SEAT THAT SAVED ME ON THE OCCASION I NEEDED TO SPILL INTO SOMEONE RESPITE OR RETREAT, HERE'S FELLOWSHIP, A SEAT RESERVED ANY DAY OF THE WEEK. THIS THANKS GIVING FAMILY OF STRANGERS, ANCIENT HALL BRIMING WITH INEBRIATED COMRADES, A CHEERS TO YOU:

BAR

OUR RAI EN

Jeppson's MALÖRT LIQUEUR

THE TAMALE GUY

got hundreds in an igloo
cooler. hot & dense. stuffed
with queso & peppers, pork & corn
delicious & delivered to dingy bars
littered across Chicago's last late night.

THE TAMALE GUY
a hero of sorts. unknown to the masses
unmasked & cloaked in dimly lit dives
weaving thru packed houses & some sad
scatterings of last calls in flak jacket flannel
dodging failing elbows & mixed drink condensation.

THE TAMALE GUY
appears from thin air.
the dust & bustle of Western Ave.

THE TAMALE GUY
feeds the multitude: hipsters & punks
artists & waitresses, after midnight
denizens who need a break & stiff drink
& something to soak it all up.

THE TAMALE GUY
must have a family, some army who helps
him wake & resuscitate for this 2nd hustle.

THE TAMALE GUY
might carry mail by day
or punch buttons & a clock
in a factory. might live in Pilsen
& wander the south branch of the river
near Ashland on the weekend & watch
fishermen lure smelt.

THE TAMALE GUY
lures the hungry, feeds the drunk
for a couple bucks.
the poor after all the pours.
he's there in the lonely of night.

THE TAMALE GUY is there.

DRIVE BY IN HUMBOLDT PARK

it's may & crisp.
an apple. the sixteen-inch
softball players wear long sleeves
beneath their insurance agency
sponsored jerseys. there's a light
rain. a grey canopy
of sky. you are
hungry. luckily Humboldt
has fried food stands
with warm meat in the windows.
Lucy is the Puerto Rican
woman selling *empadillas*
not *empanadas* she says.
her smile a secret
she tells everyone.
she puts a shishkabab of chicken
& tostones in yr hand
like a popsicle. hot sauce & salt.
we walk near the pond
& nobody knows
us
here
&
here
all the ducks are booed up
the birds too
chase each other
call each other
with song.
even the snail shells
abandoned on a rock
at the edge of the water
are left
in a pair.

this is a drive-by
date

something quick
to see each other
& make out standing
near the field
house before you
have to leave
before you throw away
the tough bits of kebabah.

the park's so big
for a moment
you can trick yourself
you're not in the city.

this same park
where bodies were pulled
from this same pond
where Puerto Ricans fight to hold
their homes on the Paseo.

my hands are birds
at yr hip. a flurry
a hot
sauce.

Humboldt's beautiful
& changing like all
the neighborhoods

for how long
we will live

here

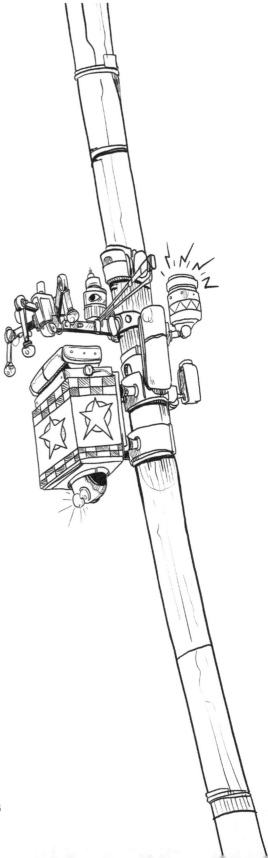

how long
will we call

this

home

song for the old bowling alley

league of misfits
the alley cat dragged in
from a night of dives & plans
abandoned. an awkward or
awesome date depending on
the number. we have to exchange
the shoes we came in with.
dismiss the mess of strings.
whites dirtied & brute. we
have to leave what we
know in order to roll, to
get what's nasty. the grime
of another's funk & feet,
the sweet meat. pick a ball
the right weight, a perfect fit or
something close to comfort. a marbel
marvel or neon magic. a rock we might
spin into turkey. grab a beer, a pitcher a
bouquet of bottles. lace up & punch the names
of the motley bunch assembled this odd night. how
we all got here a miracle of luck & endless history.
lanes rowdy or bare. lights the stark oppressive halogen
of the gig we're trying to forget or the black light 70's
bedroom your uncle prolly made a kid in. the juke box's
been updated twice. once in the hard rock big hair Jon Bon
Jovi 80's & again, in the early aughts when Nelly stormed the
Midwest like a tornado of coco puffs. this is not the roll of
Fred Flintstone. the white cave where men escape their lives,
wives or preoccupation with middle management. this is the
most radically integrated space in a city of viaducts. this is a
northside squad of Filipina doctors sippin & celebratin
out their rounds; a crew of first generation Latinx coeds
post-test at the Waveland. shout out Diversey Bowl, the
gem above the Ace hardware that went missin as condos
crept along Lincoln. the best bowler i know's a 3rd
grade CPS teacher with nails long as magic
markers, painted every night for a star trek
in the Afro-future. just one more game /
night where it feels like it's everybody's
birthday & tomorrow's a distant rumor.

ODE TO THE OLD BARBERS

there were three.
i went to the man in the middle
who knew the least english.
bulbous cheeks like cherry snow
cones. a laurel or hardy mustache.

Chicago had a polish radio station
low in the a.m., an all-day murmur.
the chatter of a different country
in a neighborhood of newcomers
when Ukrainian Village was polish
& Mexican.

black combs bathed in electric blue.
mirrors everywhere, an infinite endless
reflection. grey smocks & grey-haired
barbers who brought their lunch to work;
brown bags with pickled beets, cabbage
stuffed with sausage & rice.

the blade, exacto-knife precise, over
my ear, clip the lip meticulous, a geometric
concern. sculptors of chin, when i knew
no one else, they took me in. i told them
my bubbe was polish, *cześć,* we joked
we were cousins, though the mother
country lined her kin into pogroms.

hands of oak & pipe tobacco, hold
a knife at my throat. the sharp
gallant scent of aftershave. baby
powder on my neck like a kolaczki.
they'd send me back into the world
anew, lines sharper than the viaducts.

feelin like a million bucks for twelve.
i'd tip three, every two weeks

until the sign
says closed

& the massage spa neon
glows.

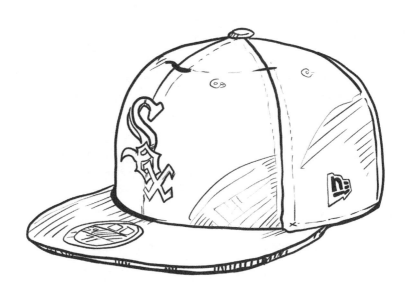

ODE TO THE WOMEN WHO CLEAN MY UNMENTIONABLES

Yesterday, I retrieved laundry / cleaner than bells,
unmentionables / caressed by another's / mother's hands.

Samantha Thornhill's "Ode to Gentrification"

my greatest luxury, sweet ladies,
                    you fold my drawers to fit
perfect in my drawers. a prophetic calculus
a measured plotting. i'm one of what, hundreds.
you're one of three, depending on the day
i get it all together in the off-white laundry bag
after a night of too many or too many nights.
you know i prefer boxer briefs & grey sheets
& v-neck white tees. you smell me at my worst.
what is the condition of falling in love with your nurse.
you allow me to come behind the Smurf-blue door
separating customers from the cash register
& soap store of travel-size tide & bounty.
i one arm heap a sack of soiled mess
onto the scale like we're at a carnival. i'd like to win
you a prize & always walk away with your fluffed
treasures. i hear of your sister Marie, your daughter
Maria, your husband who never takes you out cuz
he too is too often working. in the few minutes we have
before i pay & step, i love you like the city; fleeting
& forgetful & you love me like the city; so long
as there's pay. but every week or every other week
or anytime i can get it together i'm consoled by knowing
every garment on my body's caressed by your hands.

New Construction

the old two-flat could hold three families
or ten. inspired by the Palazzo Medici
the bungalow dream of the middle class
carried across an ocean by an italian
with good hands, a dedication to detail
& the love of laying mortar. tuck-point
with fine white lines, irregularly long
& rectangular prisms of red or gold.
sturdy like the lie of the economy. the two
flat; a family to live & a family to rent
or a whole crew of aunts & their kids
from some country not Chicago.

now there's pop-up brick veneer.
cookie cutter lego mansions that stick   out
like newcomers on the old block
who can't shake up with the corner
boys the right way & wear sweaters in summer
around their necks like herbs. boat shoes on yachtless islands.
the workers rushed & underpaid. merely bricklayers
not masons. no art or health care, just rapid profit.
a few days to erect a home. viagra condos.
bricks different. the old were heated
in the kiln for days. stood for centuries
resistant to the hawk & murderous
downpour of spring rain. now they're porous
nuevo riche, grey sponges that leak.
ACME boxes by the truckload. a cinder
fabrication. a luxe forgery. Louis Sullivan
rolling over in a pauper grave.

BUILDING A NEW
CHICAGO
☆ ☆ ☆ ☆

fiRSt fRiDAYS

where blood & oil
used to meet, a thousand
feet meander with a map
on concrete unmovable
as bone. the area's name
whispered sent shivers
if people even knew it at all
just weeks ago. there were jobs.
old machines that made
a country then slept
in dust for decades
as moss grew from light
beaming thru a broken
windowpane every day
at the same time like a punch
clock & shone a million
atoms & hands
& dollars & quiet plans
to change this earth
no one's cared for
since the crack era.

there's a block
or five. some houses
the bank foreclosed.
storefronts empty
as a pop song.

a coffee shop became
an oasis in the desert, a fort
in a forest of wigwams.
it hangs old photos
from a friend's mfa
show. the barista

plays acoustic punk
& puts a flyer on the wall
in search of a drummer.
they jam outside one night
& the owner likes it. the weather
is light jacket right. a prospector
heard the gallery next door
has an up & coming artist
fresh from saic & free beer.
a graphic designer with no kids
& more income than five teachers
gets a tattoo in a Cholo font
in a parlor that once baked pasteles.

the city sold this lot
for a dollar to a son
who inherited properties
& tax breaks from his father
whose father also owned.

this is not the first time
wealth moved from family
to family handed down as birth
-rite & rights to the land.

this is the first friday in the new city

& the illusion is that all is free
& meant for the public to merry & revel
& walk on ground zero as cranes
circle like metal dinosaurs.

there's a booth with crystal jewels:
land theft on a necklace. a license
plate coaster maker. a driftwood
sculptor. a vinyl bowl artisan. a white
stencilist with dreadlocks portraits
Black icons who suffocated beneath

recording contracts. the pieces sell
like nostrum, like the quack condos
encircling this block of mausoleums
for the widowed & empty nesters
who want to return to the revival
after paying taxes in a school district
in the suburbs for the last forty years.

a bread & circus marketing plan
backed by big liquor & real estate
developers, the local business
council. the culture industry
writ large   as walmart.

THE REAL WORLD

Urbis Orbis closed.
light fixtures upgraded.
the windows new. the 11th season
of mtv's *the real world*, the latest neighbors
seven strangers who are not polite.
viacom production teams broadcast the death
of a neighborhood as far as transnational cable lines
could reach.

beautiful vapid twenty-somethings
famous for being famous moved in
from other states with a loft of new furniture
& disposable income. their lives incessantly
monitored without the worry of Orwell.

teachers, residents, baristas & sculptors resisted.
a coalition each night gathered in the hundreds
to protest the country's story of constant removal.

they lathered the door at 1934 W. North Ave
with red paint, a lamb's blood like Moses commanded.
a tale in reverse, the lord passing over. the choir chanting
the Southside anthem na na na na, na na na na, hey hey hey,
good bye like prayer & prophesy. an omen. until pharaoh's men
removed them; from the street, from the neighborhood
& soon too from history.

THE PRE·FiXE IS IN

nothing in the new city's organic

small batch sweet butter cream.
mustache service counter. too bothered
to barista who wants to be a millionaire.
it's so expensive to eat well. i can't find a juice
less than $12. the best bite in the world's spicy
tuna on fried Japanese eggplant. it's nicer
getting robbed this way. my mom says
the old city was scary.
the new city's small & cute.
the new city downloads cupcakes.
the new city ubers from one organic boutique
to the next.

gfc (gentry-fried chicken)

long wooden tables from the park district
painted in bright jewel-tones. feng shui walls
peppered with old news & bricolaged frames.
lines of white meat out the door for an hour
since the reader raved of non-gmo amish farmed birds
rolled in rice powder, fried in coconut & kale oils.
a 2-piece here's more than an 8-piece on 87th St.
true there's no honey-spiced kimchi on 87th St.
no apple-orange sweet potato slaw. we're a long
way from the empire Harold Pierce & his wife Hilda built
when no one would feed Black folk a quick & necessary meal
five years before ray kroc
two years before the colonel
the colonial.

Hillary's Urban Eatery

h.u.e.; coded, as in white people love brunch. invite us
for hollandaise, holidays, we will turn up everywhere.
hillary like william's wife, who just said super predator.
hillary not from the hood, but who owns here now
& sends her progeny to montessori. urban as in lone   outpost
rustic tables with pastel vases stuffed with baby breath.
huevos rancheros with soyrizo (whatever that means) & flour
tortillas. the coffee is black & strong. every server, white & pierced.
every cook & dishwasher, Brown, like the sugar
the sweet that moves white into the neighborhood.

erasure

bone clean store fronts. catwalk selfie mirrors
marching to the train. the proximity to the loop, the loot
what made here so g-ddamn attractive. stacking studios
where whole families made dinner. side streets, a mini-target.
hotels sell empanadas, matcha cafes, dog groomers, yoga boutiques.
all Division Street's a strip mall, a yogurt stand, a trend mill, a tread mall
a mote of outdoor seating & fifteen-dollar cocktails armed
with summer aperol spray. splayed.
the neighborhood neutered.
its guts removed. all the good bacteria   out
which opens the body to sickness, whiteness
whitewashed. wicker park's a quinoa wrap
a lite grain, a lite beer, a small brewery
a facsimile of what it used to be.

PioNEERS

my people always been pioneers
at the front lines of new territory.
homeless with no mother country.
a life advertised in time magazine
where rent's never an issue
& the electric's always on. a life
the country summons & carrot
sticks. america itself, a new land
a foreign refuge. our experience
from jump, different. we came
running, fleeing chains but many entered
in them. we moved freely: Maxwell St.
to West Town, North Lawndale
to Edgewater, Edgewater to Skokie.

my people always been pioneers.
carpet bag soldiers in a war
we didn't know we were fighting.
diaspora peoples with bags & endless
boxes willing to sign anything & pledge
allegiance to the myth of mobility
& constant segregation, as long as we
can put these boxes down for a minute
to feed the children. these are the fatigues
we found ourselves wearing. white
litmus tests to see how safe the hood is.
canaries in the mine, chum in the water
coyotes ushering other white bodies
across the border, holding the fence
to prospect for gold. scouts
who returned with tales of ethnic
foods & how much your dollar
will fetch in the new land.

GiVE US A PoEM

wrestling with the poetics of Muhammad Ali

i am
the last
man
standing.

 still

work
in the neighborhood.
but can't afford to live
in it.

everyone is gone
or dead
or ghost

what was ours
is mine
alone.

i stalk the streets

 still

uncertain

 who is we

 &

 who is me

I go to the girl from the neighborhood

the afternoon the towers fell.

she's a barista now
& works at Alliance
the only polish bakery
still on the block.

i step off the train, wobble
knee-deep in the soup of Indian
summer. all the bars pump well
liquor onto Division. ukrainian ones
shutter by the week. cocktail lounges
ready for takeover.

she's Puerto Rican & still lives
in Humboldt though there too
forces assemble to make families flee.

the whole city sold again
ad nauseam. a mausoleum.
she labors: lattes with soy.
white yarn bow-tied around
tiny boxes of cookies, jelly
-filled kolachkes that today
are bags of blood.

i walk past the haunted bar
someone was decapitated in
just sitting there sipping a high life
a head removed from its body.

the whole neighborhood fills with ghosts.

late summer massacre
murder capital. i have double vision
& deja vu. i have
a pocket filled with coin
a country's dead currency
she no longer accepts.

the sweet between us
tastes like metal.

there's blood in my mouth
when i speak.

EVERYthing MUST GO

we're looking for work.
looking to move out
our parent's crib, to afford
some affordable housing;
a 3 bedroom with 5 people.
something to imagine a life
of our own making.

we're 18 & 22
living for the first time
with roommates
not our blood.

we're from the neighborhood
& the one over. this one's over.
our parents split & moved
to the burbs. our auntie lives
out west.

we work at the new restaurant
your boss just ate at.

we sold his kids weed out back.

we boost & rack & claim our sister's
kid on our income tax.

we live with our producer, our girl's
girl, a giant loft of squatters, our shit
in a bag.

we got the gall to think there's something
different than life intended. we're tired
of working at the bank or grocer or business
our parents moved here for.

we drink what the elders left:
7&7s, gin & tonics, old turkey in old hats.
we're new birds trying to fly.

we drop shit like pigeons damn near daily:
styles, projects, habits, visions of what it is
& what it will be.

we're making it up.
we mash up
records & tongues.
we mess up
daily.
we step on e
w/speed
to meet molly.
we out here
stylin, glammed up
rough necked. tims
& roller skates.

we house.
we rave.

we spend whole afternoons
blunted watching cartoons
for aesthetic clues.

we know the names of everyone
who works the corner / store.

we're here to stay
until the landlord says:
everything must go

ABOUT HAYMARKET BOOKS

Haymarket Books is a radical, independent, nonprofit book publisher based in Chicago. Our mission is to publish books that contribute to struggles for social and economic justice. We strive to make our books a vibrant and organic part of social movements and the education and development of a critical, engaged, international left.

We take inspiration and courage from our namesakes, the Haymarket martyrs, who gave their lives fighting for a better world. Their 1886 struggle for the eight-hour day—which gave us May Day, the international workers' holiday—reminds workers around the world that ordinary people can organize and struggle for their own liberation. These struggles continue today across the globe—struggles against oppression, exploitation, poverty, and war.

Since our founding in 2001, Haymarket Books has published more than five hundred titles. Radically independent, we seek to drive a wedge into the risk-averse world of corporate book publishing. Our authors include Noam Chomsky, Arundhati Roy, Rebecca Solnit, Angela Y. Davis, Howard Zinn, Amy Goodman, Wallace Shawn, Mike Davis, Winona LaDuke, Ilan Pappé, Richard Wolff, Dave Zirin, Keeanga-Yamahtta Taylor, Nick Turse, Dahr Jamail, David Barsamian, Elizabeth Laird, Amira Hass, Mark Steel, Avi Lewis, Naomi Klein, and Neil Davidson. We are also the trade publishers of the acclaimed Historical Materialism Book Series and of Dispatch Books.

CPSIA information can be obtained
at www.ICGtesting.com
Printed in the USA
LVHW091522101019
633801LV00007B/133/P

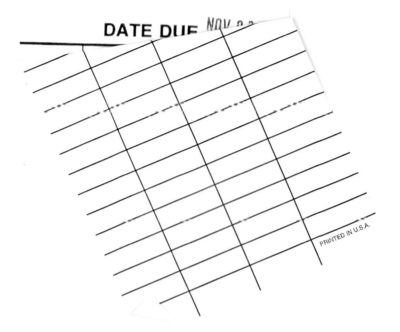

DATE DUE NOV

PRINTED IN U.S.A.